# Persephone in America

CRAB ORCHARD SERIES IN POETRY
*Open Competition Award*

# Persephone in America

ALISON TOWNSEND

*Crab Orchard Review*

&

Southern Illinois University Press

CARBONDALE

12   11   10   09      4   3   2   1

The Crab Orchard Series in Poetry is a joint publishing venture of Southern
Illinois University Press and *Crab Orchard Review.* This series has been made
possible by the generous support of the Office of the President of Southern
Illinois University and the Office of the Vice Chancellor for Academic Affairs and
Provost at Southern Illinois University Carbondale.

**Crab Orchard Series in Poetry Editor: Jon Tribble**

**Open Competition Award Judge for 2008: David Wojahn**

Library of Congress Cataloging-in-Publication Data

Townsend, Alison.

Persephone in America / Alison Townsend.

p. cm. — (Crab Orchard series in poetry)

ISBN-13: 978-0-8093-2896-3 (pbk. : alk. paper)

ISBN-10: 0-8093-2896-8  (pbk. : alk. paper)

I. Title.

PS3620.O957 P47 2009

811'.6—dc22                                    2008031313

*For Tom, always, with love and thanksgiving*

                    If her kiss
Had left a longer weight upon my lips,
It might have steadied the uneasy breath,
And reconciled and fraternized my soul
With the new order. As it was, indeed,
I felt a mother-want about the world,
And still went seeking . . .

—Elizabeth Barrett Browning, "Aurora Leigh"

# Contents

THREE

# Acknowledgments

Grateful acknowledgement is made to the editors of the following publications, in which these poems have appeared or are forthcoming, sometimes in different versions.

*Calyx*—"Persephone in America," "Accepting the Flowers I Did Not Choose," and "If I Called You River"

*Comstock Review*—"Each Spring the Bloodroot"

*Crab Orchard Review*—"A Bottle of Jean Naté," "Unexpected Harvest," and "Ruby Slippers"

*Diner*—"Trichotillomania"

*Gulf Coast*—"Forty-five This Spring"

*The Ledge*— "The Cutter"

*MARGIE*— "What I Never Told You About the Abortion," "Persephone at the Mall," and "Persephone, Pretending"

*Michigan Quarterly Review*—"American Chippendale-Style Mahogany Secretary Desk, 1845–1870"

*Mickle Street Review*—"Mud Poem"

*Mudlark*—"Jane Morris Poses for Rossetti's *Proserpine* (1874)" and "Demeter Faces Facts"

*Natural Bridge*—"Red Words"

*Nimrod*—"Ode to the Pomegranate," "Seeing the Virgin Mary at the University of Wisconsin Library Mall," and "Beauty Lesson"

*Prairie Schooner*—"Blood Elegy: Persephone at Midlife"

*Rattle*—"Blue Willow: Persephone Falling," "Persephone Remembers: The Bed," and "Spin"

*River Styx*—"My Mother and the Snake," "Persephone at the Crosswalk," and "The Favorite"

*Southern Review*—"The Addict"

*Sou'wester*—"Persephone Under"

*Tor House Newsletter*—"Splinter"

*Valparaiso Poetry Review*—"Between Green Flannel Sheets Splattered with Portuguese Roses"

*Water-Stone*—"And Still the Music" and "Biology"

*The Women's Review of Books*—"A Winter's Tale" and "Mother-Daughter Portrait"

"What I Never Told You About the Abortion" also appeared in *Best American Poetry 2006*.

"The Cutter," "What I Never Told You about the Abortion," "And Still the Music" and "Persephone at the Crosswalk" were part of a group of poems that won the Lorine Niedecker Poetry Award from the Council of Wisconsin Writers in 2005.

"And Still the Music" also appeared in *Encore: More Parallel Press Poets*, Parallel Press, 2006.

"Hospital Corners" also appeared in *Sweeping Beauty: Contemporary Women Poets Do Housework*, University of Iowa Press, 2005.

"At the Hairdresser: Persephone Reads *Elle* Magazine" also appeared in *Are You Experienced? Baby Boom Poets at Midlife*, University of Iowa Press, 2003.

"Mud Poem" and "If I Called You River" also appeared in *What the Body Knows*, Parallel Press, 2002.

"Persephone in America" also appeared in *A Fierce Brightness: Twenty-five Years of Women's Poetry*, Calyx Books, 2002.

Some of these poems appeared in *And Still the Music*, which won the 2007 poetry chapbook prize from Flume Press.

I am grateful to the Norcroft: A Writing Retreat for Women, the Virginia Center for the Creative Arts, the Wisconsin Arts Board, and the University of Wisconsin–Whitewater faculty sabbatical program for time, space, and financial support during the writing and revision of this book. My deepest

thanks to David Wojahn, as well as Jon Tribble, Bridget Brown, Kathy
Kageff, Barb Martin, Erin Kirk New, Robert Carroll, and everyone at
*Crab Orchard Review* and Southern Illinois University Press for their support
of my work and the care and attention they gave to this book. I'd like to
thank all the members of Lake Effect, my Madison writing group, without
whom none of these poems might exist. Robin Chapman and Anne-Marie
Cusac, in particular, gave the manuscript early readings that helped me
begin to think about the shape it might assume. Sharon Doubiago's epic
poem workshop at Split Rock first helped me think about these poems as a
group. Alicia Ostriker and the Master Class in the poetry manuscript at the
Nebraska Summer Writing Conference were also of enormous assistance.
I am especially grateful to Alicia, whose work on women and mythology
has informed my thinking for decades. I am thankful to my dear friend,
Cliff Dillhunt, for our joint, marathon manuscript-reading session, and to
Peg Volkmann and Julia Weaver, who keep me anchored and nourish my
heart in Madison. Gratitude to my cousins, Diana Donahue and Jean Doak,
for cheering me on at a critical moment. And thanks to Casey Huff and Pam
Gemin for their support of this work along the way.

At the University of Wisconsin–Whitewater, I am grateful to my students for
their inspiration and courage, and to friends and colleagues Dewitt Clinton,
Mary Emery, Joe Hogan, Beth Lueck, Andrea Musher, Mary Pinkerton,
George Savage, and Lynn Shoemaker, encouraging voices all. I'm especially
thankful to Pat Moran, for his thoughtful reading of the manuscript at a
very busy time. Becky Hogan's encyclopedic knowledge of myth, sparkling
wit, and unstoppable enthusiasm for this project have been a steady support.
Marilyn Annucci's poetic insight and keen editorial eye provided exactly the
right turn of the kaleidoscope when it came to the book's final organization.
The book would not be the same without her.

Holly Prado Northup, Jackie Melvin, and Judith Sornberger are my
triumvirate of muses, poet sisters who sustain the soul with their friendship
and beautiful writing. And abiding thanks to my husband Tom, for walking
with me so tenderly—in the light and in the dark.

# Persephone in America

# Persephone in America

Because the body is a map
and the because the map I know best
is the one of this country, I pluck her
from the pages of the book of myth
and paste her down here,
on a page in my journal,
in the middle of my life,
in the middle of the country,
wind from the end of a century
whistling around our face and ears.

I make her walk beside a wagon to get here.
I pick her up, like Midge or Barbie,
and say, *Listen, I know you're a goddess.*
*But those white robes won't cut it.*
I dress her the way I dressed myself
in high school so that I can remember
before it is gone—skirts
rolled up too short, white lipstick,
black fishnet stockings that left
our knees printed with diamonds.
I teach her to hitchhike
and take her to Woodstock,
skin bronzed with Bain de Soleil,
her hair streaked California blonde
the way my own once was with Sun-In.

I tell her, *In this country*
*girls grow up too young, already*
*worried about their weight at ten.*
But I take her out dancing at midnight

across the tawny fields—the Monkey,
the Frug, the Swim—all the way up
through break and line dancing,
the years humming through us
like a fast-forward film,
while she lies down with the boys
and men I remember, and the delicate,
pink rock roses of our bodies bloom and burn
but refuse to die, their petals a flag sewn
in the shape of a woman printed with stars.

I take her back. I make
her mother die when she is young
and hold her in my arms afterwards
the way I never was. I give her
a tongue, flickering like a small
green flame or a sprout of corn
in her mouth, and whisper *America,
America* in her ear while she sleeps.
I snap down the faded oilskin
Mercator projection and teach her
the names of the states, letting her love
California best for its Mediterranean air,
her feet fast in a pair of red Keds
that carry her all the way
from one coast to the other,
western meadowlark purling
a goldrush in our heads,
the history of what the body
can become here as spacious
as the sky arching above us.

I tell her the pause between breaths
is what she must always return to.
These mountains, this blue
clarity of thought and air,
golden poppies and owl's clover
blooming in clefts left
by earthquake, landslide, the flash-
fire-rape of clinical depression
that abducts us but cannot
keep us down, air breathed
from my mouth to hers, life
animating the pale white form
of a woman I walk back into daylight
with from the world below, making
of us both something greater
than loss, inscribing our names
beside those of Homer, Walt Whitman,
Zeus, and God, because it is already
the twenty-first century, and this
is America, where I say
things like this can happen.

# ONE

# Unexpected Harvest

Jefferson county resident Jim Reu found an unusual item while combining
his field recently: a wedding gown, likely from the August 15 tornado that
hit Stoughton [Wisconsin]. . . . The wedding gown is muddy and has a few
tears in it, but Reu is hoping it can be returned to its owner.
—*Stoughton Courier-Hub*, November 3, 2005

Of course it's from the tornado.
That's what we want to believe, as much
as we hope the photograph will help the dress
find its way back to the woman it belongs to.
But as the fields around town hum, rumbling
with the sound of combines harvesting the last
soybeans and corn, trucks piled high with beds
of tumbled gold, it's hard not to think it might
be Persephone's, dropped or torn off as someone
whose face she couldn't see dragged her under,
the lacy overdress ripping, its medallion pattern—
visible where the farmer and his son hold it up
in the photo—printed with mud
where he pushed her down, dark in her eyes,
dark in her mouth, dark the earth
that entered her body. Hard not to think
she might have been out there, walking
the green fields when the whirlwind hit,
her body slender as an ear of corn,
braid fraying like a tassel coming undone.
And innocent too, girl trying on her mother's
wedding dress without knowing what it means,
marriage a cave lit by fires that burn bright
then dark, so close together it's sometimes
hard to tell the difference, or understand

why joy cradles sadness in its palm, dropping it
into the ground that it may sprout from blackness.

Years after my mother died, my aunt sent me
her wedding gown, still stored in its satin-ribboned
Wanamaker's box, labeled "Mary's Dress" with peacock
blue ink in my grandmother's spiky hand.
I remember how I knelt before the box that evening,
one candle burning, making a ritual of the opening,
scared of what might fly out, afraid the dress
(which I'd seen only in pictures) might have crumbled
into dust, all its pleats and ruffles dissolving.

And how surprised I was to find it,
intact in its tissue shroud, virginal
(though I'm not sure she was), along
with the veil she'd made herself, rosettes
of lace stitched across its gauzy surface,
and the white kid slippers (a size too small
for me), still stained with dirt—
from when she'd walked across the garden
at my grandmother's farm to where my father
waited, her face radiant, exactly the way
a bride's is supposed to be, neither of them
guessing what lay ahead, cancer already drowsing
in her breast, and further down, like hidden treasure,
the egg that would become her daughter.

# The Addict

Because she is a good girl and an A student,
with a name—Charlotte (after Charlotte Brontë)—
only an English professor's daughter could have,
you're not prepared when she tells you
what's really wrong, confessing she's addicted
to OxyContin, a pain medication the paper
calls "the heroin of the Midwest,"
an opioid with the addiction potential of morphine.
And because you've watched her haul herself back
from the brink of starvation, the bulimia
that claimed her girlhood finally
overcome, you've not considered
there could be something worse,
the need for the drug so bad
she buys it on the street, taking it
to a "safe house" where she chops the pills
into powder, snorting each potentially lethal
hit through a straw or a Bic pen
for the rush she describes as "sex for the brain."
You're not ready for the startling poems
she brings to her independent study
all semester, documenting each
step of the descent, the drug like a lover
who wants her helpless on the bed, every nerve
yelping until more is the only relief,
and who cares if her pants hang
off her hips, or it takes half an hour
to piss or shit—anything to make
the loneliness fade. And nothing,
not you with your kind voice,

9

or the school, or the sound
of her father's voice on the phone,
not detox or the twelve steps
or even those unblinking poems—
lifelines that fall just short—
is enough. As she sits there,
sniffing that telltale sniff,
claiming a cold, though she knows
you know what's up, the drug
meant to kill pain killing her instead,
while she murmurs *This isn't me;*
*I'm not this kind of girl.*
Though she is and the poems go on,
compulsive, raw as the lining
of her lungs must be, as you sit there
with her, in the shortening winter light,
hunched beneath the weight of her trust,
as she slips through the blue fingers
of the world, all the things you cannot do
to save her piled up inside, useless
as the words you will later use to describe them.

# Splinter

Not down. Not underground. And not abducted, exactly,
since he calls her up and asks if she wants to come along.
A rainy November afternoon, guys playing sets of one-on-one
in a neighbor's barn after school, safety in numbers, her best
girlfriend along, though the friend will abandon her later.
Not down. And not through darkness into some underworld
of the body. But up, the ladder to the hayloft creaking
beneath their feet, the hay itself glowing, as sun breaks
through one dusty window, the dribble-dribble, thunk-thunk
of the ball and the other boys' voices receding below. Up and up
they climb toward the soft gold that smells like last summer's fields,
green she whirled through in another life, playing Kick-the-Can
or Statues with her sister and brothers. Up and up, her skin
a drum her blood thrums, each cell taut, her hand stretched
toward the boy (he is only a boy) who climbs, backlit before her,
so intent she hardly feels the needle of wood pierce her palm—
*pay attention, pay attention*—while she pushes down any
misgivings—the joking boys, some kind of cards
with pictures they passed back and forth but wouldn't
let her see. *Pay attention, pay attention.* And still
they climb. Until they are at the top and he hoists
her up into what she wishes would stay their own
fragrant realm. Forever. Not these dry kisses, this
hurried push and grab, her underpants tearing,
something that shoves and hurts, the smallest
happiness fading. Though she *is* happy to be with him
isn't she? Happy this popular boy with the loud
voice and skinny ponytail has chosen her. Happy
to walk home alone with him afterwards in the rain,
his arm over her shoulder, his black London Fog draped

around her, cloth that blots out the light of the world.
And the rain. So good on their hot skin. Washing her and
washing her the way she will later stand in the shower an hour,
sluicing the scent of him off her until the water runs cold.
Until she is something like herself again, curled in the narrow
bed of her body, legs pulled up inside her nightgown for warmth,
a pulse of pain throbbing in her palm, sliver
of wood she shuts her fingers over, makes a fist around.

# Persephone at the Mall

*Sleepwalking.*
That's what you think
when you see the girl walking
alone at West Towne Mall; *she's*
*sleepwalking,* trying on the allure
of the body like the platform sandals
and mini-skirts you wore at her age
that have suddenly come back; *she's*
*sleepwalking,* her body a new
continent she is exploring,
her breasts taut under the black
burnt-out velvet shirt,
her legs endless columns of light
spilling from short-shorts
purchased at the Gap; *she's*
*sleepwalking,* entranced
with the spell
of the body, how it drifts
on the surface
of the bustling crowd,
intricate as
the lily she seems
dressed to resemble,
the book of myths
open between her legs,
though she does not
know the story in the book; *she*
*sleepwalks,* not knowing
because she does not
see herself, does not notice

how men's glances
strip her of being, this girl
who slinks and provokes
without knowing
the danger, only
that men look and look; *she*
*sleepwalks*, and you know
that she likes it, as you did
when you hemmed your
good-girl skirt into a micro-mini
and ran to the bus-stop,
all legs yourself, nothing
touching your skin but air,
your long hair falling
around you like a veil,
while your stepmother
screamed, *Tramp!* and *You'll*
*be sorry* at your back;
*she sleepwalks*, parting
the crowds of people
before her as if this
is the first day of the world,
the mall a meadow where bees hum,
where every nameless flower
anoints her with pollen; *she*
*sleepwalks*, lost so far inside
her body you ask, was I ever
that young? *She sleepwalks;*
and it is not envy you feel
but fear—so many eyes
watching from between blades
of new grass—*she sleepwalks;*
and despite what you see,
scrying in the soot-blackened
glass of the mirror before you,

staring through the window
into you she has become,
*she sleepwalks;*
and there is nothing,
not one thing
you can do or say
to wake her.

# The Favorite

You know you're not supposed to have favorites
but can't help liking most this girl
with auburn hair, and the name of your best
friend in high school, the one who recites
swathes of Emily Dickinson aloud, standing out
like a shining blade among the bored, pasty faces
in Freshman English, announcing that she
wants to write *her* research essay on love,
eighteen after all, despite her way with language.

You don't know yet you'll be her favorite too,
happy whenever you see her name on your roster,
as you watch her hammer a house of words together,
board by shining board, turning your slightest
suggestions into windows and doors—apertures
that could open on almost anything. And do,
the day she comes to your office, an essay
cradled in her arms for you to read before
class—the one thing (she tells you)

she is afraid to write. Though she has
written it, fighting her way back inside
her fourteen-year-old self so convincingly
you can feel lilies blooming inside her skin
and the way her eyelids flutter, taste Juicy
Fruit, smell the talcumed longing that pulls
her to the carnival that night with her best friend,
flat-bellied and sparkling, looking for the kind
of boys she doesn't even know to watch out for.

But this is where things jumble and blur, her story
suddenly yours, the twinkling Ferris wheel
a circle of boys with joints you and your friend—
the one with your student's name—
found yourself trapped inside one New Year's
decades ago, the memory pushed down the way
those boys pushed the two of you from one
to another, the Beatles' "Come Together" loud
in the back of your head. As your student flirts

down the midway, through the hot scent of cotton
candy and popcorn, everything about her unbearably
young, from the small, hard apples of her knees
to the way her braces cage the sweet red
of her mouth. To the moment you know is ahead
when the boy she shunned a few steps back grabs
her arm, then yanks her under a tent flap,
the way a boy pulled you under the stairs
at that basement party. Pushing her down the way

that boy pushed you, his friend there, too, and another,
then more, then you fighting free, and somehow
your girlfriend underneath them all while you
tried to think how to make it end, *Come together,*
*right now* playing over and over. Or is it
that carnival honky-tonk, sweat and beer and
sawdust and dope, the short skirt pushed up,
the boys' movements jerky and sharp?
Because you got away didn't you, hitch-

hiking home in the dark with your friend,
who couldn't talk about what happened?
And they didn't—your friend, and your student

who was held down, the secret of it clamped
deep inside like a terrible pearl. Until this week
when she sat in her dorm and typed
what you read now aloud. So she can see how clear-
sightedly she reaches back and puts her arm
around that girl, washing her off, throwing

the torn skirt out. So she can know
it was not her fault, the most beautiful
room in her whole house built from the ugliest
mud, terror a blue vowel that kisses
the hurt. As you read back to her
what she has written, thinking of your lost
and silent friend, the iodine-sting
of your student's words burning,
healing, alive in your mouth.

# Spin

I don't remember if the bottle was a Coke or a Fresca,
just that the glass was cool against our hands
in the warm, empty tool shed. Where we'd gathered
after swimming all afternoon at Debbie Worthman's
eighth grade pool party, everyone's skin damp
and blue in the shadows, the boys' chests bare,
the other girls wearing cute, peekaboo cover-ups
that matched their demure suits. And me with a frayed

blue shirt of my father's, its tails tied fetchingly
around my first bikini, a homemade job I'd stitched
up in pink and red paisley from a Simplicity pattern,
the bottom half barely on because I'd used old elastic.
I don't know what Debbie's parents thought when we slipped
away, leaving the pool. Or whose idea it was as we trudged
up the hill between her father's prize-winning roses,
their scent filling the air like primitive attar,

their metal name tags chinking in the breeze. That seemed
to have come up from nowhere, pushing at us with invisible
hands as we locked ourselves inside the half dark
that smelled of wood chips and compost, our eyes dilating
like cats', faces suddenly pale beneath Coppertone tans.
I wasn't sure why I'd been invited to this party
or why I'd come, except that *he* was here, the boy
who'd pushed me into the pool more times than any other girl,

and who, when the guys "rated" the girls during a lull
in Mr. Tallerico's "Classical Music Experience,"
had given me a "9," Beethoven's boom making me feel

almost good enough, almost deserving of his attention.
Which, when it fell on me, when our eyes caught
and locked, threw out a taut, silk line that hooked
my breath and heart as easily as he made jump-shots at games,
the ball teetering on the orange rim—then bingo, in.

While the sweaty mascot pranced in the moth-eaten tiger
suit, and cheerleaders scissored their perfect legs,
and I'd held my breath, hoping he'd look my way, his hand
dribbling the ball as if he were touching my body.
All that, pressurized and pushed down inside as someone
twirled the bottle and it spun, blurring as we held
our breath like fourteen-year-old yogis and (thank God)
it pointed at someone else. From whom I had to look away

as her lips met his, my stepmother's injunctions—
*Don't stare; cross your legs at the ankles*—loud in my head.
Though I would have liked pointers, one dry, chaste peck
the year before from another boy all I had to go on.
But I gazed down until the bottle whirled toward me,
its opening like the little "oh" of surprise that undid
a slipknot inside my body, something not quite desire,
but what I'd soon call anticipation, singing along

with Carly Simon's song, a fist in my solar plexus
opening and closing like a luna moth's wings.
As he moved across the circle and tilted my face up,
his palm cupped beneath the curve of my cheek,
then fastened his silky, Doublemint-scented mouth
over mine, everything in the room disappearing
in the plush wriggle of his tongue, the slight
thrust of his cock stirring beneath cut-off jeans.

And my tongue moving back. As if I had been born
knowing this, as if we were back in the pool,
his hand water on my skin, the rest of the kids gone,
the inside of my eyelids spangled with paisley swirls.
As I leaned further and further into this kiss that would
sustain me all summer, practicing for the next one
with my pillow or the fleshy part of my palm, enlisting
for life to the lure of the male's hard, angular body,

the taste of mint everywhere like clean, green rain.

# Biology

For some women ovulation can be felt as a cramp on left or right
side of the lower abdomen. The phenomenon is called *mittelschmerz*
(literally "middle pain").

Daffodils and narcissi were the first things
we dissected in ninth grade, assigned
before the earthworm or fetal pig
because they were simple, nothing
but a long green stem with a blossom
bobbing at one end, the star shape lush
and strangely erotic, the scent like a drug
for a fourteen-year-old crazed on hormones
I'd memorize names for then forget
when we left the exam.

"Cut the stem lengthwise," Mr. Barrow instructed,
up to the place where seeds swelled, the bump
of ovary under the blossom like a small
pregnancy I hadn't noticed, forcing bulbs
in bowls of pebbles at home or gathering
handfuls of flowers that lit the March yard
like tissue-paper stars. After that,
we were to slice through the blossom,
copying down what we saw in our notebooks,
labeling the sepals, pistils, and stamens
that stained our fingers with pollen
the color of curry.

I did what I was told, wielding the scalpel
while my lab partner, Sean—whose cock I'd
grasp in the cornfield behind my parents'
house a year later—watched, cracking jokes
about my scientist father, calling me
Mrs. Frankenstein or Alison "Kildare."
It wasn't hard, though the stem gave
like green flesh, unexpectedly
tender beneath the blade. Even the flower
was easy, though it hurt some to mar
its cupped perfection. But when I slit
the ovary and saw the seeds—packed dense
as shad roe or a clutch of doll-sized pearls—
I couldn't stop staring, the pain in my side
sharp as if I'd cut myself with the knife,
the whole scene jellied and swaying.

Until I found myself in Mr. Barrow's chair,
the ammonia sting of smelling salts sharp
in my nose, head between my knees while
the room steadied, the place where I'd
gripped the scalpel burning my hand,
the flowers tossed in the trash as after
a wedding or funeral, and nothing
the same again, because I'd seen
inside something it seemed we weren't
supposed to see, the world insistent,
deepening whether I liked it or not, no matter
how many times I copied over my lab notes,
no matter how many long, deep breaths I took.

# At the Hairdresser: Persephone Reads *Elle* Magazine

Each year the models get younger
and younger, disappearing when you look
at them sideways. Beneath the silvery, bubbled bonnet
of the hairdryer my auburn hair "processes,"
my whole head covered with a sticky paste

the color of raisins that covers any stray
grey strands and brings out my natural red highlights.
"Grey-Be-Gone," my hairdresser calls it,
though in truth it seems no different
from my stepmother's Lady Clairol,

*hair color so natural*
    *only your hairdresser knows for sure.*

My hairdresser knows. I flip through the pages
as the models parade down the spring runways
in Paris, New York, Rome like exotic birds
about to take off in clothes no real woman could wear.
Once there was a time when I could make a skirt

from a yard of fabric. Pink velvet, one New Year's,
and a shadow-striped white voile bodyshirt
that showed slats of shining skin, my ovaries
bursting like ripe figs with their plenty.
Now, erratic hormonal buzzes—wasps trapped

inside a storm window in winter.
Everything dies. And I know some of these models
starve for a living, their angular, nearly hipless shapes
a reminder of my own, my finger down my throat in high school.
Then out of nowhere, my grandmother's beautiful

ravaged face the last time I saw her alive, the high, rouged
cheekbones and delicate skull shining above the arthritic
wreck of her body, until the room where she lay on her chaise
lounge of rose-colored silk seemed to glow and we weren't
anywhere but in our bodies—my aunt, my grandmother, me—

the red in my hair the same as the red had been in theirs,
the young woman I still am leaning toward them (as for a moment,
these models lean from their glossy pages toward me),
breathing while the world breathed with us, understanding
for the space of a heartbeat, time's sweet and invincible secret:

that everything repeats, and we watch it. We watch it.

# Persephone, Pretending

Madison, Wisconsin

When the news said that the girl
who had been missing almost four days,
only to be found in a marshy area
at the edge of our medium-sized city,
was faking it all along, I wondered
what made her do it. I'd seen
her face—bright smile, dark eyes—
on a flier masking-taped to a pillar
at the airport the week before,
felt the involuntary frisson
of the curious, then only fear
at the thought of a girl *abducted*
in this place once voted
"America's most livable city."

She must have wanted
something she couldn't name,
that good girl with good grades
who looks like so many girls
in my own classes, but who keeps
changing her story. It happened
here; no, it happened there; no,
*I really just wanted to be alone.*
Then she turns her face away,
tired of telling her tale,
not sure what to make up next
or where invention will take her.

"Fictitious victimization disorder,"
*Time* magazine claims, but I wonder
what else, imagining her in the marsh,
cold, unrepentant, powerless, her mind
gone muddy with lack of sleep,
no way out of this lie she almost
believes, or the lies ahead,
nothing but memory of the rope,
duct tape, cough medicine,
and knife she bought at the PDQ
with her own cash, wanting
to be taken by someone so badly,
she takes us, she does it to herself.

# The Cutter

*Razors are like silk,* she tells me.
They slice the skin so smoothly you hardly

feel them going in. The bread knife
is different, its serrated blade more

work, a hack saw going back and forth; there is
time to think what it does, chewing at you,

the ragged fringes of skin peeled back
like something left by a shark.

Broken glass, on the other hand, has its own
atonal music, the wound it leaves jagged

as a badly lipsticked mouth. It makes
a mess, she says, describing the scar

hidden under her clothes, the one
her mother wouldn't let her get stitched up

because she wanted her daughter to remember
what hurting herself looked like.

Though scar tissue, the girl reminds me,
has no sensation, can only whisper,

its tight, white mouth pulled shut, grimacing
around the ghost of pain, though even *that*

reminds her she is alive, is breathing,
is what cutting is really all about.

And the sestina she has been asked to write
for another class forces it all into a song,

like the kind you hear in a music box,
playing over and over, contained, though

this one doesn't stop or even slow down
at the end, but keeps going (she is

telling me all this, lifting the lid)
as we sit in the circle of lamplight

in my office, heads bent over the beauty
she wrings from her trouble, the pen

as scalpel, salve or bandage, words
blooming like blood on the page.

# What I Never Told You About the Abortion

That it hurt, despite the anesthetic,
which they administered with a long needle, shot straight into the womb.

That they hit the vagus nerve the first time and I fell down when I tried to stand.
That after the second shot my legs snapped shut—

instinctively as any wild mother protecting chick, kit, cub.
That I held the hand of a young Hispanic nurse and wept

when she said, "You know, hon, you don't have to do this."
That I believed I did, though I nearly got up and left.

That the doctor was crude, saying (when he saw me conscious),
"It's always the ones who want to be awake who should be put out."

That dilation and curettage is exactly what it sounds like:
opening, scraping, digging out a scrap of tissue that clings.

That mothers both create and take life. That I crossed a picket line
to get into the clinic. That I wanted to come back another day

but knew if I left then I wouldn't return. That my mind was not,
as I let you believe, made up that night at Planned Parenthood,

the positive lab slip shining in my hand like a ticket to heaven.
That this was where the deep root of sadness began to take hold.

That I stood in our bedroom a few days before the "procedure,"
my blouse open and bra undone, looking at my breasts, marveling

at the way they swelled, even at eight weeks, like fruit I'd never seen,
remembering the rise and fall of my mother's body as she nursed my sister.

That I felt *inhabited* then. Incarnate, the cells of my skin glowing,
bright and scared. That I wished we were married, though it seemed uncool.

That I wished you'd said, "A baby? Let's do it!"
instead of "It's your body. You decide."

That it was all surgical and neat, not even
any blood afterwards on the Kotex that made me feel fourteen.

That I dreamt of it for weeks. That we married years later, that dream
torn between us. That I had wanted to feel the hard bowl of my belly.

That I believed it was practical—you in grad school,
no health insurance, me the one with a job.

That the table I lay on was cold. That there was a poster
of a kitten dangling from a tree limb, with the words "Hang in there, baby"

on the ceiling above me. That I turned names
over and over in my head like bright stones:

Caitlin, Phoebe, Rebecca, Siobhan.
That the nurse wept with me, like some twentieth century,

Southern Californian fate, midwife to death
in her uniform printed with flowers.

That she wrapped my hands in her navy blue sweater.
That I described the thumb-sized embryo inside me in all the obvious ways—

shrimp, peanut, little bud-wanting-to-open.
But not baby, never baby.

That I saved the paperwork as proof I'd been admitted
to the college of mothers. That I told you a good story,

letting you believe I believed I might not be able to write with a child.
That this was the beginning of the end of us.

That though we are kind now, and always cordial when we meet,
a decade after our divorce, it is the one thing I cannot forgive you.

That it has taken me twenty years to find words for this story. That no matter
how many *thats* I write, there are not—will never be—enough.

# A Winter's Tale

All semester, the young woman whose mother
has been sent home with terminal ovarian cancer
comes faithfully to my 3:45 section of Freshman English.
She never says much but sits quietly in the circle,
both there and not-there, her cinnamon-freckled
face scrubbed blank with fatigue and sadness,
as we plow through the hero and heroine's journey,
the elements of fiction, a five-page essay due
every other week. She laughs just once, the day
no one's read the text and I make them act out
the version of the story where Persephone
chooses to leave—Josh, a gruff-voiced, black Hades
from Milwaukee, Scott and Brent his snorting steeds,
Kelsey and Heidi pretend-flowers, withering
under Demeter's wrath, as Kara cries, "Save me,
Mother, save me!" and is carried away down the hall.
Only after class does she tell me how things stand—
her mom moved from wheelchair to bed
and off medication, hospice workers poised
like a band of strange angels. It's the beginning
of winter, light sucked a little farther each day
into the womb of earth's darkness, the same time
of year my own mother died. As Ruth and I walk
up the stairs to my office, the ghost of my girl-self
follows behind, braids tangled, knee socks slipping
down, her violin case banging against her knees.
I've told Ruth a one-sentence version of my story
so she'll know I understand hers, said she doesn't
even need to attend class, just turn in the papers.
Still she comes, bearing her grief in her arms

33

like an invisible baby only she and I can see,
saying, "The routine helps me stay on track."
I remember how it felt to walk through the world
that way, insides empty, bones filled with air.
I want to tell her she will survive, that her dreams
of marine biology can still come true, but those aren't
the words for now. All I can do is hug her briefly,
as her mother is too weak to do, brush her hair
back from her face, and send her home, telling her
"Skip the last paper. Your mother is your most
important work now," the girl in braids standing
so close beside us I can almost feel her breathing.

# Demeter Faces Facts

No matter what you do, the kid's a girl looking both ways,
isn't she? When you really think about it. When you stand

in her shoes, whether they are the open-toed gold sandals
of Greek myth, Indian water-buffalo slides of your youth,

or those sequined flip-flops that are new again
this year, dangling from her slender, silver-toe-ringed foot,

while a tattooed dragonfly dries its blue wings on her ankle
as if she were the first to ever dream it. No matter

how she dresses, she's still your girl, isn't she,
standing between worlds, looking both ways, forward

and back, like you taught her to before crossing a street?
But deciding by herself. And you're her mother.

When you braid her hair, brushing out the night you know
she's taken inside her, picking bits of leaf and dirt

from the long, sun-streaked strands, your fingers
tangle, catching on the knots of all she hasn't said.

And won't say now, her lips sealed against you,
no matter how tempered your greeting or sweet your kiss,

no matter how tender your maternal ministrations.
Without quite intending to, she's gone underground,

the face whose curve you shaped with your own hand
fugitive, a sullen stranger's you'll never touch the same way

again. Still, you keep brushing and braiding, separating
the strands and binding them together again, as if they were

a rope by which you could hold her, tethering her to your body
as she was once anchored and fed, your blood hers. Before

she began crossing the street without looking back to catch
your eye. When you were still everything she needed.

# TWO

# In the Luray Caverns: Persephone Writes Home

Do you remember, Mother, when we took that trip to the Luray Caverns? I thought the underworld was beautiful then. It was so cool down there you pulled us kids close as we crossed a bridge over the underground river where blind fish swam with no need to see their way in the darkness. Water dripped everywhere, and we marveled at the shapes it made—organ pipes, balconies, nests of eggs in stone—all pink and green and purple in the tinted pastel lights.

But because I kissed your cold forehead as you lay in your coffin, because I stepped forward when my siblings pulled back, because I was the oldest and dutiful daughter, I am the one caught in the dark throat of the caverns, falling like those drops of cold water into forever. A stone girl dripped into a woman who only sometimes breaks away, reemerging each April into crushed purple petals, the joy of sun on my skin.

And always you ask what I ate in that place where there are no tours and the party lights have been turned off forever. And always I assure you it was nothing but the small red seeds someone whose face I couldn't see slipped under my tongue. I swallowed them because I was hungry and they glistened with the blood of the world and were sweet in the darkness. Though I cannot say if the man was father, brother or lover—slippery avenue of stone that swallows the green above.

Everything a girl encounters when she leaves her mother young, when she is left by her mother, her cheeks smeared with salt and ash. And no one to lay an arm around her shoulders. No one to tell her what it means or point the direction home through these winding corridors. This veil of darkness that swirls down around my face so that I can't see anything clearly, but navigate by touch, searching these tunnels for love's suspect but necessary embrace, the father's bedclothes frozen around me like draperies of stone.

# Mud Poem

It was the coolness
that drew me,
one hot summer evening
when, aged seven
and a half, I
knelt down
under the uplifted
arms of the maple
and dug a bowl
in the earth
with a spoon
from the kitchen.

It was the heat
that pushed me down,
like a young animal
searching for solace—
and a fascination
with texture—water
from the green
hose spurting
into the soup
of mud.

Mixing and kneading,
I felt the earth
rise and move
beneath my fingers,

slippery and elastic
as a loaf of black
bread in the making.
It was the first time
I think I saw
it was a live thing,
a creature like myself
that breathed,
foaming and bubbling
at my wrists until
just stirring the darkness
was not enough.

It was then that I plunged,
dipping my arms in
past the elbow and humming,
coating my skin
with a sheen of brown
that cooled the fever
of play, reflecting
me back to myself
so that I threw off my clothes
and began painting
my body, every
inch of me covered
in the guise
of the forest—
my head lathered,
my limbs dripping,
my torso plastered
and unrecognizable
with a cast
of fragrant mud.

With twigs in my hair
and a cape of vines
swirling behind me,
I danced
on the bare ground
under the maple.
I sang over my brew
till my head swam
and my blood tingled,
and dizzied, I lay
down, my cheek
pillowed by that
which clothed me.

And when my mother
saw me and cried out,
alarmed by my passion,
I washed it off.
I acquiesced, obedient
beneath the hose she held,
watching while the brown
rivulets turned to silver
before disappearing
in the ground.

I submitted to soap
and the scent
of Cashmere Bouquet.
But that night
as I slept, my
wet braids
tucked like tails
in the wings of my shoulders,

it was mud I remembered,
and the pleasure of black earth.
That moment of pure light
when I was the land,
feeling its skin
as a part of my body,
loving it, knowing my home.

# A Bottle of Jean Naté

... the mysteries emerge from the
private and even secret world of female experience ...
—Helen Foley, *The Homeric Hymn to Demeter*

My mother smelled like this
when I was a girl, though I must twist
the cap on the bottle I bought at Walgreen's
to remember the lemony amber, suspended
in woody florals, she'd splash over her body
after a bath, laughing, repeating the ad
that urged women of the early 60s to
"tingle at the touch of Jean Naté"
and "glow from head to toe."

She did glow then, the way the living do,
as she lay in the bathtub, stretching
a long leg to turn the hot water faucet
with her toes, no cancer yet, her small,
blue-veined breasts high and firm,
covered shyly with a washcloth
when she saw me looking, studying
the map of who I might become,
so I could understand what it meant.

I sat there, on the closed lid
of the commode, playing with the black
velvet ribbon around the bottle's neck,
sneaking glances at the mysterious
world of her body, talking about things
I cannot remember. Though my body does,
and precisely—those summer afternoons

44

she stood beside me, wrapped in a Turkish
towel, splashing cologne the color
of Pernod or celadon across her neck and arms,
then splashing me, dabbing a bit behind
my ears, the cool, green scent
rising around us in a cloud—tingling,
glowing, the body's private story
hidden but not quite gone.

# Beauty Lesson

*One hundred strokes a day* was what my mother
demanded, undoing the ribbons that bound my long
braids and running her fingers through the ropes
she'd woven that morning, binding them so tightly

the roots of my hair had seemed to tug at my brain
as I'd leaned into her body with each crisscross pull,
balanced for a moment, then swaying, my head filled
with the faint, rose scent of Cashmere Bouquet

that surrounded her like aura. Night was a different
story, my hair loosed around my body in a drifting,
silken veil she worked with her boar bristle brush,
starting at the bottom to remove any tangles until

the brush slid smoothly through, then pulling
in long, even strokes *(one, two, three, four)*
from my scalp to the ends as if she were rowing
a boat single-handed through the sea of auburn

strands *(twenty-six, twenty-seven, twenty-eight)*.
It was our ritual at the end of each day, this
brushing that prepared me for sleep as I stood
before the mirrored Victorian dresser as she had

as a girl, my head pulled back by the force
of each stroke *(thirty-three, thirty-four, thirty-*
*five)*, my eyes half-shut, hypnotized by the motion
of her hands, anchored in the rhythm the brush made

*(forty-seven, forty-eight, forty-nine)*, like a swimmer
at the end of a lifeline. As she curried and groomed
me like a filly, as she ran her free hand behind
the brush (*fifty-one, fifty-two, fifty-three*), rough

as a mother cat, spreading the natural oils, smoothing
down the strands, explaining that this was what a woman
did if she wanted beautiful hair (*sixty-four, sixty-five,
sixty-six)*, her own blonde going gray from cancer

that would take her two years later. Which is why
when I brush my hair each night nearly half a lifetime
away (*seventy-six, seventy-seven, seventy-eight)*, I
think of my mother, and how she pulled my young life

against her dying body, holding me close, binding
and releasing my hair, brushing and brushing
till it shone, stars of blue static crackling
around me like the Milky Way *(eighty-one, eighty-two,

eighty-three)*, in that chilly farmhouse room that somehow
became a small boat on an ocean where everything
rocked and swayed, where she told me what she knew
about being a woman *(nighty-seven, ninety-eight, ninety-nine)*.

# My Mother and the Snake

I had seen the snake before.
I had watched the copperhead unwind itself
from the gut and leather bindings
of a pair of snowshoes that hung on a sunny wall
in my father's woodshop, though what
it was doing there, I do not know. Another time,
it slithered away from the woodpile,
what at first seemed a nest of dead leaves
unfolding in one smooth rope of molasses
and honey. Its scales sparkled in the sun
as it paused to look back at me, the topaz
eyes so unlike anything I'd ever looked into
they froze me with their cool enchantment,
like a girl in a fairy tale who forgets
who she is, a small bell at the back
of my head chiming *poison, poison,*
until I turned and ran.

I don't know where the snake came from,
or how it found its way to my parents' farm,
just that my mother feared it, as she feared
for us kids that summer, running half-wild
in woods and field, as cancer spread its slow
venom from her one breast to the other.
I feared it too, but abstractly,
its danger coiled like the secret
of my mother's illness in some
dark crevice of family.

Until the afternoon the blunt,
wedge-shaped head rose,
hissing from the grass
where the sprinkler spun
silver over our bodies, and my mother
whirled in out of nowhere with the ax
from the wood pile, like some
avenging goddess, chopping
and chopping—my gentle mother
whom I'd seen save a choking chick,
turn a birthing lamb, nurse baby rabbits
with droppers of warm milk—
hacking and hacking at it.

Until the writhing, bronze ribbon lay still
and she pulled us close, tears
running down her cheeks, and sent us
to bring stones to pile on the body,
while the sprinkler twirled on,
dissolving the snake's blood
with water from our own well.
As if it were not the beginning
of the end of a world, as if what I saw
written on my mother's face was not
the story of just how many ways
there are to be taken.

# Persephone Remembers: The Bed

for X.

It happens in the dark.
If it were light would she be able to stand it?—
her father's bed a cave she crawls into
when she wakes, forgetting, then remembering,
the scab sleep weaves over the raw place torn open.

*The bed, the bed, something that happened in the bed.*

Her mother is dead
and everything green has been folded away,
like the flower-sprigged eiderdown in the closet
where she buried her face to remember summer
and the scent of her mother's live body.

*The bed, something happened in the bed,*

and the bear she once pretended to be—
those times she touched herself where no one had before—
has gotten inside her father's body, touching
where she touched, and it is wrong then
gone between her fingers and

*the bed, the bed. Something that happened,*

something that wakes her after she has fallen
a long way through darkness into dream and someone
who shakes her, says to get up and return
to her own bed, it is morning now, "our secret,"
she must not tell her three little sisters.

*The bed, something in the bed,*

where her mother taught her to make
hospital corners, where she tucks
and folds the blank spaces into rhymes,
counting the beats between each breath,
*bed* and *head*, *bed* and *red*, *bed* and *dead*.

The bed, the bed, *something happened* and her mother

is dead, and there is no one between
the girl and the sparks of her father's
sadness, loss a bright red wound he circles
like a bear before sleep, the cave walls
flickering with the prints of his hands.

*The bed, the bed*, it is

her own bed then, carved mahogany posts
and pineapple finials, the mattress
imprinted with the shape of her body,
and she is a feather, light in her father's arms,
though what she remembers is a dream

*the bed, the bed,* girl moving like a ghost,
just a glimpse of *something*
*that happened* to that girl in green
cotton pajamas; she is that girl
*in the bed* with her father then

back in her own bed again, where the pictures
run together into something wet on her leg,
*the bed* and the bear and *what happened?*

It blurs, it is red, and she is her mother,
which must mean she is dead too,

though sun shines through white lace
across her window, though her small
sisters sigh and stir, though she tastes
the dirt from which each green word springs,
bitter as medicine at the back of her mouth.

# Hospital Corners

Because it was the first thing
about housework my mother taught me,
and because it was all I knew to do
those blank weeks after she died,
I made my bed every morning, drawing
the rumpled sheet flat and tight
from the top down, then making hospital
corners, folding it in the neat,
diagonal V she'd learned in the Red Cross
and showed to me. She'd made it look easy,
flicking the linen she'd bleached
with Clorox and hung to dry in sun.
And it was when we did it together,
our hands moving in tandem
as I copied her movements,
the pleasure of doing what she did
all I needed to feel useful and real.
Alone by my maple spool bed,
I'd move from one side to the other,
pretending she was there,
until she somehow was, the January
room brimming with light
I had no word for but *angel.*

Together we'd draw the top sheet up,
turning the hem side down in a neat
cuff over the mohair blanket,
then pulling the spread smooth,
pulling it back and up and over
in a kind of envelope that held

the pillow, slapping the fold
straight with the edge of our hand.
We folded the rose-printed coverlet she'd
made for me last, in accordion pleats
I could unfurl in one smooth line,
as I got into bed at night and lay there,
mussing the taut sheets
with the tears and sleep of the living,
waiting for morning when she
would come again, calming me
with those simple, familiar motions
that melted the world and dazzled me
with their brightness, making it possible
to do something almost like going on.

# Finding Hell on the Map

It is easy to imagine hell in the wrong place,
human to want to make it something real
or geographical, a landscape we can point to on a map.
The San Andreas Fault, the Luray Caverns,
or that spot in the Hudson River the Dutch called
World's End, because the currents there pull you
down in every direction. Who wouldn't want
to place it outside the body? Who wouldn't flinch
from conceiving of it as something carried inside,
weird baby everyone births—men and women
both—swaddled in an indigo scarf, slung
just beneath the heart. Who would want
to admit that sometimes, when the baby is lonely—
for hell is the loneliest place—it crawls
inside the heart, prying open the red shells
and curling up. Like a pearl, or a parasite,
or a monster torn from a medieval drawing.
It's normal to look for it outside.
Who would want to carry such a creature?
Who would want to harbor such sadness, admit
such raw need, offer such hot, red succor?

## American Chippendale-Style Mahogany
## Secretary Desk, 1845–1870

Because it came from my grandfather's bedroom
it intimidated me at first, dark and brooding

as he was, his Irish melancholy saturated
with cigar smoke and the scent of Scotch whiskey.

Already old when I knew him, he spent each day
in his "library" downstairs, the book-lined lair

where he read the *Irish Times* and worked the entire
*New York Times* crossword puzzle before he strolled,

whistling, "dee-dum, dee-dum, dee-dum," down the Persian-
carpeted hallway, the clink and gurgle of the crystal

decanter against a shot glass all that interrupted his tune.
Each afternoon he drove away in a long, black car

to the Philadelphia Cricket Club where he did something
important, his work running the Doak Woolen Mill—

where his immigrant father began as a "picker" at ten—
bequeathed to warring sons who'd ruin the family business.

I couldn't imagine what he'd done at this desk,
its stained finish black with time, except pay bills,

and so planned to do the same. Or what he'd stored behind
the twin glazed doors until I unpacked the leather-bound set

of George Eliot's novels, *Romola* inscribed with the words,
"Bought on our wedding trip to London, November 1908.

This eased my sea-sickness, coming back on the Lusitania."
Or stumbled on the map of the family farm—where my

mother had married—stashed in the secret compartment.
Or found the silver-framed photograph of my golden haired

mother herself—his favorite daughter—standing on the beach
at Mantoloking, New Jersey, her legs as long as the world

must have seemed the day he snapped the shot, the paper
cover on the back torn away, the words, "Mary to rest,

December 17, 1962," scribbled like a private message
I found two decades later, as I unwrapped this gruff man's

grief and tenderness from where it lay, hidden beneath
the broken-arch top with rosettes and a flaming urn finial,

the things he couldn't say written down, love's shorthand
warm and red as mahogany beneath its dark, Victorian stain.

# Seeing the Virgin Mary at the
# University of Wisconsin Library Mall

Someone has drawn her portrait in pastel
on the sidewalk, filling a whole square of concrete
with her face as if the stone were paper.
I see her upside down, must swerve to avoid
stepping on her hair as I rush across campus,

late for a panel where I'm supposed to talk
about writing and healing, some vague idea
about my mother, dead these many years,
as muse of poetry clutched inside my manila folder.
Her name was Mary too, and since I wasn't

raised Catholic, I couldn't help but mix up
the Queen of Heaven and my mom, whose name
means salt and bitter, and who became a kind
of saint in our family because she died so young,
her faults smudged pretty by memory's thumb.

She drew with pastels too, and I think she'd like
this face I turn to regard, suddenly so mistily clear
on the sidewalk that for a moment I think she's
a vision, like Guadalupe who weeps for us all.
But when I look closer, I see she's just a girl

whose clear, surprisingly hazel eyes catch mine
and look back, as if she sees the world inside me.
She could be Afghan or Spanish, Irish or half
black, her skin soft and gold as the apricots
that grew in my California yard, the barest

suggestion of a mantle floating around her, blue
as creek water, blue as loss, blue as my mother's eyes.
Which gaze through time from mine as I worry
over what I can really say about writing and healing,
the pains the world gives us adamantine,

indifferent as nature. Last night, I read
that the word "heal" means "to make whole again,"
though I think we are more broken as we go along,
our rough edges startling in their complexity
and beauty. Years ago, a friend sang *La mer*

*est ma mere, is my mother, is me,* her sheared
velvet voice spreading a cloak of comfort around us,
as Mary is said to do, protecting the world
from God's cold judgment. I don't know
who drew this girl, warm on stone, where many

pass and see her, can't say why she moves me,
except that she seems like family, gazing back
from this fleeting and secular gallery
where she'll soon wash away, like a sand painting
or Tibetan mandala, her colors blurred

then disappearing in the first autumn rain,
impermanence the lesson we must learn over
and over. And though I'd have done anything to keep
my mother alive, the blue surcease of Mary's mantle
was wrapped so gently around her it was impossible

not to notice how many places light lands, even
as we leave, or how many ways there are to believe—
in this Star of the Sea, this Mystical Rose, this Queen
of Heaven, Mother of Everything who holds the world
tightly in her arms like a wild and impossible baby.

# Mother-Daughter Portrait

A woman *is* her mother, that's the main thing.
—Anne Sexton

After the anthology of stories and poems by women
who were girls when their mothers died was published,

complete with black and white photographs of each
writer as a child, pictured with the mother who would

so soon be gone, people kept saying how much I looked
like you. It was something I'd wanted to hear my whole

life, as I'd stared into mirrors, trying to see beneath
their silvery surface and through the ghost-body I seemed

to inhabit into who was really there, and what an "I" was
anyway without a mother to guide her. And while I'm glad

my friends see our resemblance, noting the upward tilt
of our mouths, the tiny lines rayed out around our eyes

when we smile, and even the shape of our eyes themselves
(though Jenny has your smoky gray), their exclamations

make me uneasy. Instead, I apologize for how you look
as I never did when you were alive, saying, "She was already

dying when that picture was taken; you should have seen her
when she was young." Or noting things that can't be seen

in the picture, both your breasts gone, your dark blonde
hair threaded with grey. How the blue dress you're wearing

is the one you'll be buried in, looking so much older
than your forty-two years. But people keep insisting on how

alike we are. And I keep pushing that likeness away, as
even now, I sometimes push comfort away when it's offered,

the way I hugged your sawdust-stuffed Scottie dog
after you died, a little more of it spilling out each day,

no one there to mend the tear, the shape things make
disappearing what I know best, after all. Even as I walk

through this bright world, winter sun shining on my hennaed hair,
ten years older than you will ever be, looking so much like you

that when my aunt takes my face between her worn palms,
searching for the you in me, it hurts. And there is that moment

when I pull away, as every daughter does, leaving behind
whatever your sister almost sees and walking quietly off,

stepping over the stile into the wild meadow—
the one where you never walked, the one you never

even knew existed—that has, all along, been growing
into the picture of who I became without you.

# The Meadow

Often I am permitted to return to a meadow.
    —Robert Duncan

We all go there eventually,
taken by the dark god from the green
meadow life must seem as one is departing
toward another meadow, where it is always
night, though we like to think
(don't we?) that there is something
light there, if only glow-in-the-dark
stars the gods have painted or pasted
on the ceiling of that world so that
the place where we reside forever seems
a bit like home. That is, if the soul
has a home without the body. Sweet
body, that rots or burns behind us,
body it is hard to imagine—as I sit
in this bright room, sun warming
my hand as it moves across the page—
ever being without. As if the soul
were smoke or a wisp of fog, something
we can't contain, that moves over
the meadow, touching everything lightly,
weaving itself lightly into every strand
of grass, though we'd like to pin it down.
Life is a story about the soul, after all,
unfashionable as that sounds, hard
as it is to say in the twenty-first
century with the force and solemnity
it deserves, repeating the word *soul*,
the way Sappho said, *lyre, lyre, lyre,*

the words dancing together on a scrap
of parchment like music,
fragments meant to be memorized
even as they are sung.

# THREE

# Jane Morris Poses for Rossetti's *Prosperine* (1874)

He wanted to paint me.
Though I was married to his best friend,
I felt his eyes follow me everywhere,
his gaze like a sable brush on my skin.
He undressed me, though it wasn't me
he wanted at first, but the way my body
arranged itself under my clothes, my bones
and muscles struts for the teal velvet
drapery he wrapped me in. And my hair,
of course, that cloud of auburn
I loosened, coppery strands
floating around me like opium smoke.

I could tell right away he enjoyed
making me pose, his directions godlike
and stern, as he moved me about like a doll,
saying, Turn this way, now that. Look back
at me over your shoulder as if I were the last
person alive. Now lift the pomegranate
with one hand, but clasp your wrist
with the other. As if trying to stop yourself
from eating something forbidden.
As if you are offering it to me.

I must confess it bored me, standing
that way for hours, hand bent slightly back,
neck arched and aching. I did what he said,
lifting the fruit he'd slit with his penknife,
its skin pulled back like a scab to reveal
the wound's garnet-pebbled surface. It was even
my idea to press my mouth to the seeds, staining

it red, the tart juice puckering my lips
into that downward pout he loved                .
because it was sensual and sullen.

I stared back at him from beneath downcast
lashes as he painted, my eyes the color
of my robes, knowing he wanted me before he did,
desire before it's admitted an animal
that doesn't know it ought to run, every
moment ripe fruit about to be broken open.

I stood there before him for hours, tendrils
of ivy brushing my cheek. I stared
at him as he stared into me, pulling
out a sulky darkness I hadn't known
I owned, the brush rarely still on the canvas,
the scent of sweat and turpentine
and oil paint filling up the room.

I was so good at keeping still
you could hardly see me breathe
as the brush slicked across my skin.
I made time stop, the way it's supposed
to in art, that auburn hair I'd later
drag across his body merging
with the shadows of the other
world looming there behind me.

But though I may have seemed his prop
or plaything, some *object* he arranged,
like the sticky fruit bought fresh each day,
the footed brass dish, or the mirror
behind me, reflecting light from the world above,
we both knew I *was* Prosperine,

flesh and blood frozen in time's chipped
gilt frame. He couldn't have painted
the picture without me, my eyes on his,
their teal green gone almost black
and taking him down, pulling him under
into the sensual muck, everything about
the underworld different than he'd expected.

# Forty-five This Spring

All this year I have secretly been growing old,
the ovaries spilling their last burgundy stain,

dark as wild blackberries I plunged my hands into
twenty summers ago, heedless of scratches.

They've been shutting down when I wasn't watching,
closing up shop while I plotted the possibility of a child

at mid-life, estrogen's gunpowder line disappearing
fast as dust in rain. No hot flashes or night sweats,

no blood-flood breaking the uterus-dam,
nothing but me and this sputtering body

that still fits, even betrayed by the moon.
Dark veils slide across her farthest silver reaches

like mirrors in a house where death sits down
and visits for a long time before leaving.

Oh moon! Oh Hecate, gate-keeper, cave-dweller,
one-who-knows-her-way-in-the-dark, goddess

of crossroads and young things, why must it end?
I fold up names of children inside me—

Erin, Elizabeth, Beatrice, Shihreen—
the way my sister and I once folded antique

baby clothes we found in a trunk in the barn,
as if they came from another life too precious

to be worn in ours. Their syllables follow me
like small ghosts; they cling to every thorn.

# And Still the Music

in memory of Josie Avery, 1953–2003

One month after your death,
and I'm doing my every-other-day-when-I-don't-run workout
at Curves for Women–Stoughton, Wisconsin's
equivalent of a gym—where I've already
won a "Curves buck" for guessing tonight's
trivia question, and the big news
is that the local Wal-Mart won the best
"hometown store" award, and the ladies—
as they call us here—are sweating and panting
their way through the circle of machines
when "Great Balls of Fire" comes on
and damn if you aren't right there before me,
the slit between worlds opening and closing
like an elevator door as I hustle
from the pec-deck to the recovery pad,
and for just a second, for a breathless,
high-stepping, hip-swaying, triple beat
second, I see you, dressed in that vintage
purple lace you wore to a dance in college
almost thirty years ago, waving a rhinestone
cigarette holder, your arms open, your mouth
red and alive, startling me so I almost stop,
until I see that if I hesitate, you fade
and that to keep you here I have
to keep moving because you never
sat any dance out; and so I do,
powering my way through the leg press,

the oblique twist, and the knee squat,
until my muscles burn, moving my arms
in and out, up and down, running nonstop
on the pads, singing under my breath
with the music, which somehow becomes
"R-E-S-P-E-C-T" and then "Great Balls of Fire"
again, and every good dance song that dumb college band
called Widespread Depression played, the sweat
pouring down my face as I dance with you
in this room full of middle-aged women
trying to stop time or at least hold it at bay—
and who wouldn't cry?—as I dance with you,
as if my good heart and lungs could somehow
bring you back—breathing life into you the way
the heart-and-lung machine could not—in this room
where you both are and are not, and the music
keeps going, and I remember you twirling once
at a dance and saying, *I'm happy, so happy*, as if
you could have died then—and still the music
carries us, and tears splash down my arm
for the girls we were together and the women we became,
for the empty place on every dance floor without you.

# Red Words

for Judith Sornberger

There is a red place inside
I am trying to get to.
Not red-red.
Not the poster paints
or Crayolas of childhood,
but something deeper, more
primary, something sweet
but tinged with the hint
of black
burning in the sumac's
fiery brand, the shadow
pebbled
on the pomegranate's skin.
Something like menstrual
blood that begins
fresh and arterial,
before darkening
to a shade I barely
recognize as mine.
Something that almost
isn't even blood anymore
but a substance
oxidized.
Something
that tastes of rust.
Something changing.

I used to wonder
how it could possibly
come from inside me
(though I knew it did),
imagined the world
on the other
side of my skin
marked with prints
of hands red as
the maple leaves
falling this morning,
the ones I stride through
on my power walk
around the park,
my blue and silver Adidas
breaking open their color
so that the scent rises,
older than I am,
older than time
in its incalculable passing—

these leaves like ones
I collected
and pressed between
sheets of waxed paper
as a child, taping them
against the watery
blue panes
in our farmhouse,
that for a few days
lit them into
stained glass before
the scarlet faded.

As it always does.
As it must.
Though it returns
each autumn as surely
as the sun rises across
the rose and silvered fields,
as surely as poems do
after silence—red words
from a red place
on my red tongue,
the whole, bright
fruit of the world
ripe again, ready
to harvest, tasting
of red as I praise it.

# Between Green Flannel Sheets Splattered with Portuguese Roses

All night, in the middle of winter,
the great horned owls call around our hill,
their *who's awake, me too* drifting
through the bare branches, soft as smoke,
soft as their loosely packed feathers made
to move through air without making a sound.
Now, in the burnt down nub, in the raw beginning,
they are mating, the murmurous calls flung out
in lassos of sound that seem to circle
our house as we lie awake, eavesdropping
on this primal call-and-response, this avian
love song. As if it can tell us something
about ourselves as we curl, impossibly human
and other, in the nest of our bed.

When we first moved here, I thought it seemed
a hard thing, mating as owls do, in the dead
of winter, their eggs laid in February or March
in a nest stolen from crows, great blue herons
or hawks. I pitied the female, protecting
the brood as the wind tore through the oaks,
wondering how she kept warm, though I knew
the male fed her. But now it makes sense, not
lonely at all but ferocious as they are,
and mated for life, winging through the dark blue
air, the country night powdered thick with stars
one cannot see in the city. The owls can hear
a mouse moving beneath a foot of snow,
and their eyes close from the top down, like ours.

Though they are not like us at all.
Though it is our luck to lie here,
overhearing the way the male calls out
in his low voice and the female answers,
the *I'm here, I'm here, I'm here* not
so different than when we call *Whoo-whoo,*
*I'm home; where are you?* whenever we enter the house.

You doze, falling asleep so quietly
it is as if you are moving through the air
on the owl's soft wings. I lie awake,
listening, straining to hear each *whoo, whoo,*
*whoo-whoo* in a way it seems I have not done
since I was a child, listening as the Perkiomen
River purled outside my bedroom window.
That was before I knew sadness, before
anything I'd ever known had ended, before loss
piled up inside me, a mesh of fur and bone.
And this is now, my life still large
with all that lies ahead, here, in the middle
of winter, in the middle of the country,
in the middle of the years I have been given,
all my wandering having brought me to this:
our warm bed and your breath, steady beside me,
the owls' beautiful and incomprehensible
music floating over our sleep.

# Blue Willow: Persephone Falling

Depression is hidden knowledge.
　　　—James Hillman

You think it will never happen again.
Then one day in November it does, the narrow,
dusty boards of the trapdoor you fell through
twenty years before cracking apart, a black grin
opening its toothless mouth, darkness seeping out
to fill the dead cornfields rattling around you.
That sound's back in your head again—
like bees or static or rubber bands
breaking. And beneath it a distant hum
you remember being scared was voices
till the doctor explained it was your own brain,
working overtime to understand its disordered signals.

And meanwhile, every sadness on NPR is yours—
from the African country where 30 percent of the child-
bearing women have AIDS, to the Appalachian mother
who sells her great-grandmother's Blue Willow china
for fifty bucks to feed her kids, to your own
mother, who dies again every autumn, something
wrong when she didn't come home for Thanksgiving
the way she promised, the torn-sheet dinner napkins
you'd embroidered—"M" for "Mommy"—with ordinary
thread, wrapped in tin foil under the bed, melancholy's
blue index finger pressed into your forehead, choosing
you for its team. Where you must play for life,

whether you want to or not. Though that's not
what you're thinking as you hurtle

through the night, jittery as the rabbit
you swerve to avoid, your head filled
with chattering fog, a glass door sliding shut
between you and the world, that feeling of being
outside yourself so loud you don't seem real.
Though you are. As you maneuver the car carefully
through the dark, remembering how you willed
yourself to live this way for two years,
synapses flashing like emergency lights
you thought you'd never see again.

But here they are, the medication you've ratcheted
down for a year necessary after all, the biochemical
net too small, the darkness you've pushed away
for twenty years with what your doctor calls
*one hand tied behind you* suddenly back.
As you remember setting out your mother's
Blue Willow on the table every night
as a child—blue people in blue houses
under blue trees—each plate a story you can
walk into, where everything is fine. If it weren't
so dark inside and you weren't so scared.
If you could only think how to get there, and what
treasure you are supposed to find when you do.

# Trichotillomania

You know when it started but not
how to stop, though you've played every
behavior mod trick, and now try Celexa,
the latest pink pill, rumored to block

exactly *this* urge—your hand to your hair
for so many years now since that first
strand, pulled out by accident
in Mr. Sinapi's eighth grade U.S. History,

days after Joe Mortola sat behind you,
running your braids through his hands.
You didn't know you were *anxious*,
couldn't have described the neural itch

that tripped the switch that makes
you do it over and over, depression's twin
a monster that makes you into a monster,
ancient grooming behavior meant

to calm, but left behind
by evolution and run awry.
Or is it the way one grandmother
washed her hands raw,

and the other, like you, tore
at her own hair until there were times
when there was no more auburn,
only a tight wig, marcelled waves

that hid the scabs and stubble
coming in, the disorder passed down
like blue eyes or being left-handed?
It is like weeding, this search

for the bad thing, ardent plucking
that sometimes remits for years,
only to return when the world presses in,
pulling the one thing that calms

the buzz in your head, though *it's
crazy, it's . . . crazy,* worse
than your stepbrother's drinking,
your sister's cigarettes.

But the therapist says, *It's all
so-o-o biochemical,* this secret,
this stigmata, this visible wound,
weird disorder no one really

understands that turns your body
into a force you must resist,
as if some other woman stands,
balanced on anxiety's saw-toothed

edge, her fingers
tangled in your hair
like a lover's, running each
strand between forefinger

and thumb like a connoisseuse
of silk, caressing it a little
before she tears it out
at the thick, black root

that always grows back, stubborn
as the imperfections
she believes are rooted
so deeply within you.

# Accepting the Flowers I Did Not Choose

Not the yellow mums, their heads shaggy as small lions. Not the purple ones either, so regal, surely Persephone's flowers in their deep-gentian darkness. These were the ones I wanted, the ones I envisioned on my doorstep beside the pumpkin and maize, or before the blue-black mouth of the fireplace, their color illuminating the hearth. But only the rust-colored ones were left, the skin-of-the-pomegranate colored ones, the ones with petals the color of the strand of blood and uterine lining I saw in the toilet this morning.

Thirty years of blood. But I still catch my breath at this cycle that goes on without a single thought of me but that *is* me all the time. Even now, in my middle years, in this time-before-the-time-of-change, when life moves through me as quickly and as surely as this season, with its endless fields of wheat and bronze and gold does, every morning this week glowing like something out of Keats's "Autumn."

And yet the body is extravagant still, emptying its granaries and coffers as if there is no end. As if there will never be an end. As if it had nothing better to do than ripen another egg, send it on the way. And if that one isn't taken? If that one isn't pierced by the arrow of a single, swirling swimmer? Well, there is always another up there in the cinched-velvet countinghouse, in the small, wild plums of the ovaries that continue producing, the way a tree I once saw did, even beside an abandoned farm.

And why not be extravagant, spendthrift? Why not fling eggs, flowers, time itself away? Isn't is all fertility? Isn't it this unending commerce with life and death, standing at the turnstile between the two worlds we must all inhabit, with seeds flying and bright days in the wind? With the cornfields shining, and the cattails, and the red-winged blackbirds that flash up like ebony commas, their epaulets the color of blood lit by sun.

Isn't that the all of it, and isn't that enough? The fields around me shining and shining until I want to weep, speeding west on County N, 20 miles over the speed limit, singing "Oh What a Cryin' Shame" with the Mavericks, and weeping for joy and grief at what one life will gather in its arms: my mother dead so many years beneath the soft earth, the depression like black ice that nonetheless lets me live, and my husband, who lies down beside me as if our bodies are the first meadow in the world and will glisten like this in the sunlight forever. Like these mums the color of rust, the color of pomegranates, the color of the blood-stained torches the roadside sumac lift from their blazing nests. The ones that are still there after all the leaves have fallen. The ones stubborn and sturdy enough to keep their color all winter.

# Persephone Under

In truth, winter's the season I like best, though I would never
have said so before descending that narrow, rocky trail,
all the flowers in the world winking out behind me, nothing

but a few kernels of corn clutched in my hand. Before that
it was impossible to imagine what it's like down here,
though I sometimes tried as I fell asleep, the doorway

into dreams wavery as old glass, the mattress a boat moving
beneath me. But it was nothing like this permanent stillness,
even the sound of the river we all must cross like black silk

slipping under ice. No wind in the bare oaks, no moon, no stars.
Nothing but this hearth, its red core glowing like a forge
where the world is made. Up above, life pulses on.

Girls wash dishes, get their periods, brush Maybelline
onto their lashes. The lines in their faces deepen as they marry,
have children, their lives twisting and turning like yarn

in my mother's hands, the fruitful earth an endless
round—green breaking from each seed in tiny flames, bees
everywhere, a frenzy of apple blossoms falling into grass

like snow. Mother's so angry I left she's gone on strike
and hidden her face, a nanny incognito at Eleusis, busy dipping
that stupid boy in the fire. As if she could ever replace me,

the one she turned away from for five minutes, the one
whose name means "She Who Shines in the Dark," the one the dead
reach toward, hands held out for the pomegranate seeds I provide

as food for their journey, the work of comfort mine after Hades
makes his selections. They know me for who I am—Soul Sister,
She Who Tells It Like It Is. The flame of my torch warms their faces

into small suns I cradle in my palms before I plant my scarlet kiss
and settle in, listening to their stories as they pass between worlds,
their words caught like bones in my throat: *It was as if the silo swallowed,*

*burying me with grain. . . . After all our shows together, I couldn't believe*
*he'd hit me with the knife . . . . I felt the bomb strapped against my body,*
*beating like a heart. . . . They burned my baby first*—some hard, some easy,

each one a journey made alone. I write them in a Morocco leather-covered
book, its pages decorated with narcissi, pomegranates, and sheaves of endless
of grain, where seeds sleep, waiting to sprout again. I thrill, tracking

one word to the next, liking it almost as much as sex, though I'd never
tell him that. *Under* is the quietest room around, a place so still I can
hear my thoughts, twittering like finches in the bush outside my window

when it snowed at home, the only thing busy in this peaceful place.
The dead do not cook, or send e-mail or make love or take showers before
rushing off to work. All they do is wait to tell me their stories, patient

in death as they never were in life, art and gardens the only countries
where we get to live again, my job more like Mother's than I ever imagined.
As I listen, my pale hand with its ruby ring moving slowly across a page

that shines like a snowy field, writing a tale where we come to a house
in a dark wood and find inside it a mortal family sitting around a fire,
rosy-cheeked and warm, the air alive with the sound of human voices.

# Love's Apprentice

First cold front of the season,
and all night the black-and-white cat sleeps,
tucked under my right arm the way
he has since he was a kitten. On the left,
your skin pours out heat,
the goose down comforter floating
around us, its feathery walls a cave
where we curl against the year's
oncoming darkness, two more cats
anchoring our feet, while the old dog
dreams deep on the floor beside us.

Once we wake and talk for a while in dark,
as couples do, what we say less important
than the fact that we speak, words to describe
an ordinary day a kind of parenthesis
enclosing us, like the gold hands
clasped around the gold heart
on my wedding band from Ireland,
the emerald in its center a meadow only
we know, hidden in the heart of the forest.

Because I met you in the middle of my life
I try to take nothing for granted.
I'm ten years older than my mother
was when she died, a young woman
falling asleep for the last time
in her hospital bed, a snapshot of her three
small children cupped in her hands.

And because you and I have both
been married before this, we know
some things don't last,
no matter how much you want them.

*Don't ever die,* I said to you
last week, as we made the bed together,
your face one I dreamed before I was born.
October wind blows outside our window, the crickets
that have serenaded us all summer now almost
inaudible on the other side of the glass.
The eiderdown rises and falls, an undulating
landscape animated by breath, the heat
our bodies make together wafting back around us.

You fall asleep, holding my hand against your chest.
I lie here, thinking about how many centuries
people and animals have curled this way together,
bodies nestled close for safety and warmth,
and what a privilege it is to be alive,
daydreaming like this
in the middle of night
about all the lives we lead,
and how my arms will never be big enough
to hold the ones I love
the way I want to hold them.

Though I do it anyway,
though I open them, trying.

# Blood Elegy: Persephone at Midlife

On reading that the rind of the pomegranate is high in estrogen.

Always she has eaten of it.
Always, though a friend
informs her that the rind is bitter,
she has taken it between her teeth,
chewing it the way Inuit women
chew sealskin to make something
so soft it can be wrapped
around every secret known by the body.
She has licked it and gummed it,
taking each scarlet scrap
and stitching it to another
until she had a red dress,
though red was never
her natural color, though her
estrogen level sputters and falls,
inevitable as the gas gauge going down
in a car where she finds herself
headed straight into a blizzard,
too many miles behind to turn back now,
the road ahead a blank page,
a tundra white-out, the mirror of her own face
vanishing beneath a continent of years.

Still she moves, forward motion
the only possible elegy
for all the blood she has shed,
for what ticks through the slow,
red clock of the body, snow whispering

against the windshield of a car
one only drives alone, the body
dreaming itself into red—
wolf, salmon, fox, or even
the cardinals of her childhood,
erupting in a ring of fire
around the outstretched
palm of her mitten.

She put her hands out then
to the flame-colored birds
as if they could warm her.
She puts her hands out to them now,
though there is no one but herself
to see the tree in each palm,
its bare branches maps of a country
where the soul will always land.

Snow falls in great sheets inside her body.
The red dress shimmers and clings, bright
as the blood-stained hands of Inuit women,
the satin lining beneath each mortal
curve and cleft of her still
the world's mistress and queen.
Though the flesh continues its
slow fall away from the fruit of body.

Though she leaves the car and walks
for a long way into the dark.
Though the fans of wrinkles open
a little farther around her eyes each day,
directing her fierce, blue gaze
toward the moment when she is nearly bone,
her every surface scrimshawed by time,

the red dress her life was nothing
but scraps of bitter skin.

Why does it take half a life
to learn red and the shape of this wildness?
To become this tough, sinewy meat
that lopes alone toward the end,
looking for the pack it has lost,
refusing to lie down anywhere
near my fire and find comfort.

# Ruby Slippers

in memory of Richard Hunt, 1951–2003

I'm not looking for ruby slippers
when I dart into the Stolen Heart—the only
decent gift and home decor shop in my small,
Midwest town—searching for a valentine
to send a friend in England. But there
they are, perched on the padded edge
of a vintage jewel box, their rhinestone
bows sparkling with stars the size of sequins.
They are shiny and red as apples on the outside,
red as I imagine rubies must really be, painted
with the kind of enamel that shimmers
underneath, as if glitter were frozen
then polished to a sheen. And they're gold
inside, as if made for fairies' feet, not
some girl from Kansas. Or a woman like me,
stuck somewhere in the middle of my life,
and worn down, this grey January morning,
by the effort of holding melancholy at bay.
But there they are, real as my own hand,
picking them up and turning them over.
No price, so I walk to the front of the shop
to ask, not meaning to tell the owner
the story of you, my dead writer-friend—
how I was Dorothy and you were Oz, my words
and secrets safer with you than God, the work
of finding a way back home our perennial subject—
my public reserve broken by these small shoes
that seem to have tumbled from the sky to my hand.

Which the shopkeeper folds my fingers around,
explaining that the shoes were once really a pin,
whose tiny clasp has broken. *And I think,*
she says, smiling, *you should have them for free,*
getting out a small velvet bag to pack
the shoes more safely. *We'd just mark them down*
*for our 'broken box.' I believe they're meant*
*for you. If you ever get that clasp*
*fixed, come back and show us.*

Which is how I've come away with one valentine
and a pair of red shoes I look at in the car, washing
them with my tears, thinking about the kind
of things one does not say in poems: how I believed
in angels as a child, how I will never
have another friend like you, how the world
opens its arms to us when least expected,
making a path, lighting a fire at the cottage
hearth, creating a home where love may enter,
its small heels clicking toward us over
the flagstones, its rhinestone bows shining.

# Reading a Famous Woman Poet's New Book, also about Persephone, on the First Day of Spring

I see her point, of course, about hell
being a kind of perpetual winter, an Antarctica
of the heart that it pains Persephone to leave,
a place where nothing flourishes but the bitter taste
of chopped-off lines, a grim interpretation
the famous poet defines as *candor.* But there is more
than one way of telling the truth. And I can't help
but believe in something else as I stare into the old
apple tree opening outside my window this first day
of Blue Ridge Mountain spring, where forsythia erupts
in yellow fountains, azaleas shake out ruffled silk
skirts, and narcissi have been up been up for weeks,
each blossom a cup of scent it seems almost possible
to drink. No leaves on the trees yet; that's true.
But as I walked by the lake last night I could feel
it coming, all the edges of my body dissolving
for a moment as I touched a catkin spilling
from a branch whose name I did not know, the tiny
chartreuse explosion attached so delicately it broke
beneath my hand. *Surely this is the way to live,*
I thought, in pursuit of some kind of mercy,
believing green will come again, even when it departs,
falling to earth, leaving us guilty about keeping one leaf
from what it might have been. And perhaps it's naive
or romantic, but this morning, gazing into the apple,
trying to mark exactly where pink turns into white
(as if seven drops of blood had been stirred into
a pail of milk to paint the outer shells of each petal),
I surrender to the idea of return, to the belief

that people, places, things do come back, happy
to be here—even if we cannot see them the way
I see this flowering tree, or the way we want, even
if changed from what they were—the war between winter
and being alive the oldest one there is—a honey-scented
insurrection, a pyre of white fire these open petals
resurrect, as I lean toward them, trying to transcribe
again the great and ordinary mystery of being mortal.

# Asparagus Season


first green it is always
the kitchen
bright stalk in the middle of
so much wanting
I do not know
when it starts
but it does
start
tender as
buds
pushing the dark earth
of my childhood
a door that swings
backward and forward
and always
my mother
the farm
and her full hands
those large
baskets of giving

she offers shoots
furled spears
tentative as
the shape of my own legs
on the white
path of her garden she
sings of song
life breaking the crust
of the black earth
cracking the deep
mounds of our silence

97

believing it all
I cook asparagus
brief in its season
it is the briefest
but fierce as
lit candles
or the promise of rain
in each forkful
I lift rain
and the shape of this wanting
that is so green into
a beginning
a garden
an open mouth

# Each Spring the Bloodroot

What did I marry
when I married the earth
but the life of the body?
Earth opened like a wound
in the body and the one
who takes what he wants
when he wants it rushed out
with all his black horses,
the sun the smallest lamp,
extinguished in the wake
of his passage.

He took me.
He took me down
to the lowest level
of the world
with his body,
that remains forever
embedded in mine—
coal star, obsidian knife,
broken pieces of a mirror
shrouded in black silk—and me,
dressed like a bride on her way
to a funeral.

He took me.
And sometimes
he takes me again,
knot of dark limbs
tangling with mine

only last week
when the man I love
came into my body.

I held him.
I held him where he fit
in the center of the pomegranate,
in the middle of the world
that is dark and sour and sweet
at the same time.

I held him.
And he held me.
But a dark figure
lay briefly between us,
and the girl buried
in the earth of the body
that is my body called out.

Silently,
the way the ground does
when you break into it
with the shining
tip of a shovel.

I was nothing then, *nothing,*
my mouth a slit opening
and closing on air.

Nothing.
Then everything,
the tenderness
of my man's hands
as he touched me everywhere

calling me home
to the life of the body,
pressing me gently back
inside myself the way my mother
used to press earth down
around the flowers
called bloodroot
she transplanted
each spring
to our garden.

# Ode to the Pomegranate

after Gerald Stern

I'm eating a pomegranate for breakfast,
though it means I'm standing at the sink
and tearing the fruit apart with my hands,
though I'm leaning, hunched over like an old
woman, to keep the juice from spurting on
to my white flannel nightgown and staining it
like blood from the virgin I was thirty-seven
years ago, *that* brilliant red surely fraught
with some alchemical meaning the world
has long forgotten. I'm eating a pomegranate
for breakfast, and tasting its peculiar mixture
of promise and regret as I stare out my window,
which is dirty and smudged and hasn't been washed
in at least three years, though my neighbor
does hers once every season. But this doesn't matter
because I am eating a pomegranate, which is high
in antioxidants and will help me see through the dust
like Superwoman into the world of white. Where snow
has fallen overnight on the abandoned garden, full
of tough, blackened beans, desiccated tomatoes
and herbs that return, green in their season.
Six months from now, I'll stand out there and eat
a ripe plum tomato sprinkled with sugar or salt,
the way I did as a child, poking my hands
between the fragrant, furry leaves, searching
for the perfect one the way I've read saints
searched for thistles. But now I am eating
a pomegranate, fruit of winter, fruit of lust,

fruit Hades doled out to Persephone, seed
by sparkling seed. Which is how seduction
happens isn't it, a bit at a time, unbearably
slowly, until you want to jump the bones
of whomever you desire, your muscles liquid
and woozy with wanting and waiting? Some
say the apple in Eden was really a pomegranate,
and this morning, juice running down my wrists,
endangering the ridiculous white eyelet frills
and ruffles at the end of my sleeves, I am inclined
to believe that version of the story, tart and sexy
and probably a lost chapter in the Gnostic Bible,
still buried somewhere in a jar in those war-torn
deserts where pomegranates first grew, common
as apples in Wisconsin. And meanwhile the juice
runs into every crack and crevice of my hands
as I lift its tartness to my lips. Queen
of pomegranates, queen of fruit, plant which grew
from Dionysus' blood. No wonder Persephone
ate what Hades offered. Who could resist
the thought of being marked with such red,
the way I am marked when my husband kisses me
during blood time, then works his way back up,
my white skin printed with roses, the iron taste
of my own blood there between our lips. Oh,
pomegranate, that brings it all back as I stand here,
shivering in my bare and callused feet,
munching and crunching the mysterious seeds
between my teeth, thinking of making snow angels
etched in red, or drizzling pomegranate juice
in a bowl of snow the way my mother spilled maple
syrup, making candy. In Greece you can buy
a silver pomegranate on a chain to wear
around your neck, and I wonder, is it holy,
would it save me? Which might seem sacrilegious,

though I don't intend it that way. It's just
that I'm eating this pomegranate for breakfast
and thinking strange and wonderful things,
its juice like an astringent drug that won't
take me anywhere but into my body. So no wonder
I'm thinking of Eve and Persephone and all
those other wayward girls, wanting to be one
forever myself. Oh, pomegranate, shipped
from California and plucked from a bin the size
of a small closet at Woodman's after infinite
deliberations. Oh, perfect red globe I picked
and eat, messily at my sink, swallowing sunlight
from the Golden State in the middle of winter,
swallowing desire, swallowing knowledge (for who
wouldn't want to know everything there is to know?).
No wonder Eve picked you and Persephone ate,
letting herself be persuaded by the gleam
in his eye, tearing back the pebbled skin
that bursts with seeds, in such a hurry she simply
couldn't wait. Oh, pomegranate, that tastes
of life and death and longing for what we cannot
name, greatest and most complicated of fruits
that brings me to this place, my hands
stained red and sweet as I eat, slurping up
your scarlet elixir until I am sated,
and the world begins again inside my body.

# If I Called You River

for my husband

If I called you river and straddled
the silky silver muscles of your passing.

If you called me river and pulled me to you, swimming
in the silky, silver pull of my legs.

If I wove myself around you, sweet
and sinuous as water itself, as the call
of the redwing floating toward you now from the cattails.

If you slid beside me, sleek and playful
as the otter careening down his muddy ride
in one long breath before he caresses the water.

If I caressed you back, reflecting sunlight,
reflecting wingspan of hovering red-tailed hawk,
reflecting the tenderness with which light
is received always by water.

If you were water entering water.

If we flowed that way for a long time,
distinct but inseparable, the glinting
flecks of silica from your sediments mixing
with the sun-sparked mica of mine.

If the spring rains came, pushing us hard and fast,
from our home in the mountains.

If I had known high water and times of flood,
the edge of me lapping, leaving a birth-scar
along a line of rain-drenched trees.

If you had known those times too,
your calm surface churned into a wall
of water pulled, root to stem, stem to leaf,
leaf to air where it balances for a moment,
quivers, and falling, begins again.

If I were a river you had never seen
but had dreamed of forever.

If you were a river I could taste in my sleep.

If even in winter we kept moving together,
meeting in secret beneath our glassy quilt.

If everything is season and snowmelt.
If everything is release and return,
the peppered foam of frog spawn
and the salmon's muscular
silver thrust.

If I called you river.
If you called me river.
If the river knew anything more
than this sweet braiding and undoing of water,
that feeds everything
and yearns for everything and is,
in its rushing, everything the river can know.

If the river knew.
If river were ever possible to contain.

If the heart were, and the blood, and the body,
this human urge to name things
by things other than what they are.

I name you river.
I name myself river.
I name what we are together river
carving a channel between the grassy banks,
leading us

to the open mouth,
the salty swallow,
the deep, green voice of the sea
that cries out so far within us
I cannot tell if it is you who cries out or me.

# Persephone at the Crosswalk

She could be my daughter,
this girl with corn-silk hair—
like mine at her age, but prettier, neater—
who stands on the other side of the street
with a stack of Nancy Drews this sticky
August day in Stoughton, Wisconsin,

waiting, like I am, for the light to change.
Which takes a minute longer than it should.
So that we stand here, regarding each other,
a woman in mid-life, and this girl, her legs
like spears, so delicate and untouched she
hardly seems *real*, everything about her

perfect and young, from her cut-off
blue jeans, to the way her lashes curve
on her cheek, to her body, wrapped tight
in itself as an ear of new corn.
I'm on my way to the library; she's
headed home, the books I imagine

she'll spend the afternoon reading
tucked in one arm, all she'll need
as she watches her sisters and brothers.
Cars purr past as we wait for the light,
looking right into one another,
as strangers sometimes do, with clear eyes

and kindness. It's her beauty that draws me,
but I can't say why she looks back,
except for the weight of my gaze sweeping

her body, hungry for what I have missed,
the daughter I would have had not a girl
at all but 21 now, nothing on this earth

more gone than her. Then the light clicks,
the little figure of a man blinking
bright in its dark eye, and the girl
and I pass one another, smiling.
She looks at me closely, veering so near
I almost think she'll speak, the slight

breeze of our passing just brushing
one another's skin. I don't know
what the girl sees when she looks
in my eyes, or what looks back at me
from hers, or why this street is a river
between worlds, here in the middle

of the country, in the middle of summer,
the fields around this small town rippling
with harvest, cornstalks taller than any child.
But when I reach the other side I stop
and look back, unable to leave her.
Only to see she's doing the same,

time and no-time passing between us,
tasseled and falling, as we stand here,
smiling again, then suddenly waving
before we turn and walk away,
the sun raining its yellow plenty
everywhere down upon us.

# Notes

"Unexpected Harvest": On August 18, 2005, an F3 tornado, with winds up to two hundred miles an hour, passed through rural subdivisions and farms north of Stoughton, Wisconsin, destroying nearly one hundred homes.

"Persephone at the Mall": The phrase "the book of myths" is intended to echo Adrienne Rich's poem "Diving into the Wreck."

"The Cutter": The phrase "the pen / as scalpel, salve, or bandage" is a variation on a line in *The Record of Mary Morrow* by Katherine Wells.

"Demeter Faces Facts": This poem was inspired by (and takes some of its language from) Jane O. Wayne's *Looking Both Ways*.

"Persephone Under": This poem was inspired in part by Sarah Getty's poem "A Winter's Tale," and by Carol Orlock's novel *The Goddess Letters*.

"Ode to the Pomegranate": This poem takes its form, as well as the information about saints and thistles, from Gerald Stern's "Grapefruit."

Some of the poems in this collection have been fictionalized to protect their subjects' identities.

# Other Books in the Crab Orchard Series in Poetry

*Muse*
Susan Aizenberg

*Lizzie Borden in Love:*
*Poems in Women's Voices*
Julianna Baggott

*This Country of Mothers*
Julianna Baggott

*The Sphere of Birds*
Ciaran Berry

*White Summer*
Joelle Biele

*In Search of the Great Dead*
Richard Cecil

*Twenty First Century Blues*
Richard Cecil

*Circle*
Victoria Chang

*Consolation Miracle*
Chad Davidson

*The Last Predicta*
Chad Davidson

*Furious Lullaby*
Oliver de la Paz

*Names above Houses*
Oliver de la Paz

*The Star-Spangled Banner*
Denise Duhamel

*Beautiful Trouble*
Amy Fleury

*Soluble Fish*
Mary Jo Firth Gillett

*Pelican Tracks*
Elton Glaser

*Winter Amnesties*
Elton Glaser

*Always Danger*
David Hernandez

*Red Clay Suite*
Honorée Fanonne Jeffers

*Fabulae*
Joy Katz